To Amy with love

Mom and Dad

Christmas 2020

The
Math
Campers

✳✳✳✳✳✳✳✳✳✳✳✳✳✳✳✳✳✳✳✳✳✳✳✳

The Math Campers

POEMS

Dan Chiasson

ALFRED A. KNOPF
NEW YORK   2020

THIS IS A BORZOI BOOK PUBLISHED BY ALFRED A. KNOPF

Copyright © 2020 by Dan Chiasson

All rights reserved. Published in the United States by Alfred A. Knopf, a division of Penguin Random House LLC, New York, and distributed in Canada by Random House of Canada, a division of Penguin Random House Canada Limited, Toronto.

www.aaknopf.com

Knopf, Borzoi Books, and the colophon are registered trademarks of Penguin Random House LLC.

LIBRARY OF CONGRESS CATALOGING-IN-PUBLICATION DATA
Names: Chiasson, Dan, author.
Title: The math campers : poems / by Dan Chiasson.
Description: New York : Alfred A. Knopf, 2020. |
Identifiers: LCCN 2020005027 (print) | LCCN 2020005028
   (ebook) | ISBN 9780593317747 (hardcover) |
   ISBN 9780593317754 (ebook)
Subjects: LCGFT: Poetry.
Classification: LCC PS3603.H54 M38 2020 (print) |
   LCC PS3603.H54 (ebook) | DDC 811/.6—dc23
LC record available at https://lccn.loc.gov/2020005027
LC ebook record available at https://lccn.loc.gov/2020005028

Jacket art from the collection of the author
Jacket design by Kelly Blair

Manufactured in Canada
First Edition

for Frank Bidart

Contents

The
Math
Campers

⁜⁜⁜⁜⁜⁜⁜⁜⁜⁜⁜⁜⁜⁜⁜⁜⁜⁜⁜⁜⁜⁜⁜⁜⁜

Bloom

Mural, David Teng Olsen, 2017

Through his eyes I see in the dark.
     I see through change the static.
Night says to day, *You do you,*
     then emerges bright as a peacock,

its black drapery embroidery
     smiley faces looking vaguely smashed.
Day had a state-of-the-art screen
     accentuate each pixelated daisy.

You could kill the backlit spectacle
     and use it as a mirror of the stars
or take the comfort on its merits.
     Tomorrow will be worse, it cooed.

Dave put a feeding tube up where
     the sun don't shine, the moon
going, *Did you have to? Did you?*
     then smiling to show it didn't mind.

Louis had the breakthrough moment
     on what looked to be a pizza slice:
It's the cover of your book, he said—
     Dad, it's the cover of your pizza book—

Must We Mean What We Say?

A Poem in Four Phases

She had a new feeling, the feeling of danger; on which a new remedy rose to meet it, the idea of an inner self or, in other words, of concealment.

HENRY JAMES, *WHAT MAISIE KNEW*

I

·ו·

Euphrasy & Rue

—the day my eye flew all the way
what could I see with my vanishing eye

myself looking up in wonder or
was I the woman standing next to me

it was impossible to say
it is impossible to say

where faraway was or why
we care O nigh and distant cam

held in my palm now landing
in the open zone it measured

in the open zone it measured
face-to-face: we are not strangers—

HE TOLD ME, at sunset, this October, he picked some Nippon daisies, the last flower to flower, a verb named for its noun.

He said what might have been began to come around again. He said the neighbor lit his house on fire, then blamed a meteor.

He wrote:

"The neighbor named his source.
It overflowed the sluice.
It was the nightjar's voice.
It was the daisies before frost."

He wrote:

"Another brief, interminable.
Another bombshell:
a burnout blamed for the fire
the neighbor set!"

The Perseids rejoiced, then shot themselves. A source confirms:
it was "a silent suicide."

He wrote: "Binoculars superfluous: / we saw it with the
naked eye."

He was writing on the edge of an emptiness, where everything buzzed and beckoned him forward.

It was a strange time in the country. Distrust reigned.

He distrusted his own distrust of distrust, and so went out into nature, to study things up close.

He wrote: "Confusion in the hive. Nature / Locked the door on her darlings."

News reports confirmed: "They shivered and pled and prayed / And died and were ploughed under."

He was writing an autumn journal, he wrote, because in autumn everything abundant was dying. The old themes had "proven true." A source confirms.

His own death and the death of everyone he loved confronted him on his long runs at dusk, in the woods.

He went into nature, to make a pinprick of his eyesight. He focused on small blossoming things and magenta berries at the end of fall.

Lines of poetry came into his mind as he ran: The tangled bine-stems scored the sky. An artery upon a hill.

It may just be my mind, he thought. It may just be my mind. He wrote: "It may just be my mind."

He wrote:

"In the branch overhead,
the nightjar,
the manic neighbor,
told dirty jokes.

Mothers moved their babies
to another tree
alarmed to see
how far he had fallen."

He remembered the morning of the eclipse.

He wrote:

"The sky was impossible,
then our heads turned.
The noon midnight came
it came to us one by one."

He viewed the Druidical majesty of the eclipse from the stone
steps of Memorial Church, and it was then, a source confirms,
that he knew all about New England.

A tour group passed:

"That is the—" [points to the sky]

"There is the—" [squints]

That is the eclipse of the sun as seen from the middle of a thriving city, an ancient city in the new world, from the porch of spirits and the vault of sorrows.

"The new and missing stars," he wrote.

THAT FALL, he had been invited to live, for a time, in a famous poet's apartment, among the books and objects that the poet had left behind when he died. The apartment was on the Sound, on a little V of land with rocky beaches and foggy moors, high up where the steeples and cupolas were his neighbors.

He described the light as it moved from room to room, across an eccentric palette of colors from flame to teal to cherry.

Then the darkness took the colors away, in the same sequence, flame, teal, cherry, and this happened every day.

He could read about these walls, those colors, that light, that dusk, in the poet's poems. Or he could put the poems down and look at the walls, or run his hands up and down the walls he'd been reading about all afternoon and ever since he was young, when the poet was alive, standing where now he stood.

He wrote: "I met him only once, when I was in college. He was elfin, skeletal, kind, flirtatious. His mind operated almost apart from his strange body, like a drone piloted by a faraway stranger."

Now the drone flies through time, not space. Its controller, long dead, still flies it over our heads.

A source confirmed: "His body was a stick insect, but his smile flashed the news of immortality."

Pick a flower, they said. Then choose an emergency.

He chose a daisy and an earthquake.

We had daffodils and cardiac arrest, they said.

He was struck.

Now pick a flower and a war.

The correct answer was tulips and Vietnam.

He wrote:

"In the cellar near
the bulkhead door,
where the darkroom
chemicals were stored,

there I discovered
the chamois uniform
my grandfather
kept as a souvenir."

The correct answer was violets and Korea.

*He was struck again, and his right cheek exploded upon
the blow.*

He had been a child only yesterday. He still had scrapes and cuts from playing on the cellar floor, where the darkroom chemicals were stored.

He'd been a child long ago, in a place he described as snowy, with many junipers, and many mysteries, in the aftermath of something so awful nobody would tell him what it was.

The answer was hyacinths. He had hyacinths.

He was given tea, then praised.

He was a child still. That afternoon he explored the cellar where the darkroom chemicals were stored.

He unpinned a medal from the uniform, and wore it, a corsage, on many snowy afternoons throughout childhood, in front of the mirror.

The correct answer was violets and World War II.

Half in, half out of my dream:
      deer wander in a bright auditorium.
They are serene until they're seen
      when they bolt and scatter, looking for cover.

I stand totally still on the half-court line.
      Then I move, and the deer go berserk.
A doe just split her head open
      when she rammed a cinder-block wall.

A fawn pulls all her fur apart, and gags
      on mouthfuls of hide she can't spit.
I see the hunger in their stenciled ribs,
      the furniture inside their skin.

And then I'm spared, alone in bed.
      I'm forty-six, a trespasser
in my dream gym. The deer are children.
      I'm the Maypole they dance around.

He wrote, "In my dream, I am in an elementary school. There are deer all around, looking for food. They are licking the linoleum floor and biting the wooden risers. I am standing completely still, terrified of startling them."

He patrolled the Sound in his mind, counting the buoys as they bobbed in the tide.

Every buoy was an age he'd been, every age he'd been could be found among the low-lying hulls and docks, dusk settling down, the long, empty sidewalks leading to nowhere, leading to water. . . .

Nine and thirty-one were side by side. They shared more than he had known: the correspondences were hidden under the heavy cover of chronology.

His life, he wrote, was not a line.

His life was not a ladder.

His life was not a long walkway leading to nowhere.

Here, side by side, were sixteen and four.

He wrote:

"The crickets made the silence sing.
Partiers scrimmaged on a pier.
The Sound echoed a bottle smashed.
High up, all night, I reran sixteen."

HE WAS WRITING an autumn journal, he wrote, as a bridge across time. He wanted a bridge across darkness.

He needed a string to hang his moods upon.

On his daily drives, he used a GPS that could tell him, up ahead, where the broken-down cars were, or where he would meet the police, facts about the traffic as it lurched and settled, lurched and settled, lurched and settled, into, into, itself.

His journal, he wrote, was his GPS: it showed him what was up ahead by measuring what was still behind, and figured the difference, and measured, and to some extent determined, the path he needed to travel.

He loved how, when he drove, time and space became a single entity, with the GPS locating discrete episodes, however minor, in his future.

Or not minor.

He asked me my happiest memory.

I was eleven, this was before my father died. Not long before.

We'd gone up to the farm for the weekend, I was eleven, it was before my father died; we'd gone up to the farm for the weekend, I was fixated upon the things I'd brought along, been allowed to bring along. It was before my father died, not long before.

I was eleven. My mother was parting and braiding my hair in the back seat of the car. We were not far from the Canadian border, where the landscape flattens again.

He wrote: "When you told me about your mother, I pictured a pragmatic woman with abrupt, decisive manners, a kind of commander, a person of high Victorian morals, and rigid New England habits."

By the end of the long ride, I'd finished my book. In my childhood, I told him, all I did was read. I had finished my book and dreaded the weekend without the next book in the series, which I'd forgotten at home.

Time sharpened suddenly to what was happening to me in that moment, first X, then Y, so horrible, such an exposure to death.

"Like a mirror with my face painted on it," I wrote.

When we arrived at the farm, down a long gravel driveway, past the barbed-wire sheep pasture, we scattered to our bedrooms, mine on the third floor.

I found, in the third floor hall, a waist-high bookshelf full of books I had not read.

I was eleven, this was before my father died, not long before.

Sitting in a swivel chair, high up above the Sound, he found an old book by Jules Verne on the study shelves, *From the Earth to the Moon,* and spent the long morning reading.

If you want to make it to the moon,
not halfway, all the way;
if you want to see
the tininess of all of your obsessions,

loyalty, et cetera, a speck;
not halfway, all the way;
if you want to see
love exposed as a perspectival trick;

worthwhile, worthless, what you loved—
not halfway, all the way,
a triviality—
then mind what name your master gave.

Bobbing lifelessly beside the story,
halfway, not all the way,
you stand for [   ]

He wrote: "I am working on a poem based on a Jules Verne story about a voyage to the moon, where a mascot, a dog ominously named 'Satellite,' is found dead on board the space capsule, his body dumped into space and forgotten; until the end of the tale, when poor Satellite is discovered to have loyally accompanied the spaceship, bobbing up and down, lifeless in darkness, inert in the enormous cold and loneliness of space, all the way to the moon."

The blank kept getting filled in and deleted. The final line, he wrote, was "The neither-here-nor-there which buoyed me."

IT WAS ALREADY NOVEMBER when he wrote again. The first frost ruined all the Nippon daisies, and spoiled a single holdout bright-pink starlight hydrangea.

He had arrived at a trio of symbols: the drone, which he associated with the imagination; the GPS, which connected time and place, and suggested those few places in his childhood that remained, to this day, unchanged, and which he visited when he too wished to seem unchanged after so many years; and the buoys, which bobbed independently as aspects of symptoms of the greater force, call it God, call it the ocean, call it chance, the buoys which drifted this way and that, amicably, like stars in the night sky.

The drone, the GPS, and the buoys, symbols which he said would tie his book together, ways of understanding himself in the enormity of time, his book only a sliver of the slightly larger sliver his life represented.

He had a strange and vivid dream. He was driving in the country, on winding roads near his childhood home in Vermont. In the darkness, he struck what he believed was a deer.

When he pulled over, he discovered a short, bearded man with a pointed hat, dead in a ditch by the roadside.

He knew instantly that he had killed a troll, the sort of cartoon troll who dwells under bridges in storybooks.

He piled the troll's body into the trunk of his car.

Some miles down the road, distressed by the accident, he again struck what he believed to be a deer.

When he stopped his car, he discovered, dead by the side of the road, the body of the poet Robert Lowell. He loved Lowell's work and had long fantasized about meeting him. He once asked his friend Frank, who had been Lowell's protégé, if Lowell would have liked talking to him. Frank seemed to wince, but suggested that yes, perhaps Lowell would have.

He put Lowell's large body into the trunk of his car, next to the compact body of the troll.

Some miles down the road, on an especially dark stretch of highway, he again struck a heavy object or body with his car. He stopped, and there beside the road was the body of a stranger. The stranger was a young man, perhaps twenty-five, though he was badly disfigured by the force of the impact. He put the stranger's body in the trunk of his car, on top of Lowell and the troll.

With the stranger, Lowell, and the troll in the back of his car, he drove through the night, the horrible weight of his actions settling upon him. In the dream, he was looking for a place to bury or hide the bodies; which, when he awoke, he understood to be his dream's own management of time, consciousness, and guilt.

When he awoke, there were no bodies to dispose of. But he had a dream he needed to interpret.

In the swivel chair where JM wrote, he wrote he wrote:

"In the swivel chair where JM wrote
I read an inscription
from our mutual friend: *For James,*
who is a great poet—Love, Frank."

Later that night, he wrote to Frank:

"I am in Merrill's apartment for a residency and found several books of yours on the shelf, which you'd inscribed for him in the seventies and eighties."

Later that night, Frank wrote back:

"One more world buoyed by talent and money, gone—to have what you always effortlessly found to be there, gone."

Later that night, he remembered a time in high school when he and his friends partied in the woods on a frigid March night:

"We lit the forest up fucked up!
then two by two, whoever was who,
sought out the dry and grassy ground—
bare-assed, you first, then I will follow."

Like youths in a Shakespearean pastoral, they sought out woods for leisure. But the woods there were frightening, full of ravines and chasms and gorges, and every year someone, usually a tourist, fell; and the pall of depression fell in every dark corner, and in every household of everyone in those days in northern Vermont, including, he told me, his own.

He was leaving, he said, a blank in this stanza:

"I'm leaving a blank in this stanza
until the neighbor's flashlight
peers into the heart of things:
[   ]"

A stanza, he wrote, which would be undone if ever it was done,
defeated if he ever succeeded in finishing it.

Deleted, rewritten.

Before the correspondence slowed that fall, he wrote a series of letters about transformations he had witnessed. For the first time, he told me he had two sons; he told me about changes in their lives as they grew older, and changes in his own body, as he approached fifty. These letters were somber, sometimes hard to follow, as though the pressure of transformation was too much for him to bear.

Two times he lashed out at me, for merely listening.

In one letter he claimed to know my real name, which was impossible, since I had no real name. I was the channel through which his mind passed, and then I was a gap, an absence, which frightened me.

We worried who had imagined whom, which was futile, because both of us were fundamentally unreal, like contesting realities in a film: we were held, suspended within the larger dream; we alternated coming into, then stepping out of, the light.

The letters would crest with some extraordinary insult against me, which I mirrored back at him. Then he would calm, and the calm became mine; and together we became rather tender and vulnerable, two strangers, alone together in a total, collaborative nonexistence, the happiest and safest place on Earth.

I received the last letter before Christmas. He was going home, to see his mother.

His last letter included a poem he'd written about his sons, "Euphrasy & Rue," titled after the passage in John Milton's *Paradise Lost* which De Quincy had used to describe the feeling of an opium trip.

It was never really in his power to hurt me.

It was painful to imagine that someone I had imagined had imagined me, and could simply stop, leaving me stranded, without oxygen, like an astronaut alone in deep space.

I know he felt the same kinds of fear.

It was painful to know he'd been hit, hard on the face, and then again.

Though afterwards, he was given tea.

It was pleasant to imagine him on a rooftop sunset reading about a rooftop sunset writing about a Sound sideways peach sunset across buoys and yachts.

The day all the water zippered over my father's head, I knew what being stranded was; my whole life since I'd been

(continued)

stranded, until I dreamed him up; now, since he was gone, I was gone, and since I was gone, he was gone.

"My imagination is a form of forgery," I wrote, then went to bed.

At dawn he wrote:

"High up all night I thought
 of my sons, how when they wake
 I will be finishing this poem—
 my night their day, my day their night."

At dawn he wrote:

"Birds, check. First light, sunrise.
 This pole vaulting got me down.
 My outline splayed on the guest-bed.
 Swift captive, tie me up. Bordello bait: tie me up."

Euphrasy & Rue

Years ago, our sons were born. We named them
      Iris and Daffodil. They changed,
one to Euphrasy, and one to Rue;
      to Euphrasy and Rue they changed.

To Euphrasy, to Euphrasy, to Rue:
      to Euphrasy and Rue they changed.
Years ago, our sons were born;
      our sons were born years ago.

On the stereo, we played "Over and Over"
      over and over, while all the while upstairs
they changed; we played "Over and Over"
      over and over, while all the while they changed.

One by one they replaced the days we'd made
      for them with days they'd made.
To Euphrasy and Rue they changed,
      they changed to Euphrasy and Rue.

They saw the sadness on the other side
      of the horizon, how flowers
blossom, and flash, and fade, remorse
      their daily food, and cried.

Our sons were born; the stereo played
      "Over and Over" over and over;
they changed to Euphrasy and Rue,
      and now they patrol the skies.

II

⁜⁜⁜⁜⁜⁜⁜⁜⁜⁜⁜⁜⁜⁜⁜

Q & A

Q: "Over and Over," over and over?
A: By such lures and enchantments is time stopped.

Q: What part or season of the creation is *Tusk*?
A: It starts time over; new dream, repeat, new dream. . . .

Q: As to the creation: where is its refresh button?
A: In a star, in a stock car, on Orion, in the mountains.

Q: My heart is anguish. How can I vanish it?
A: O vanish isn't a transitive verb.
   The song is coming on again: Listen.

[Silence while the song plays.]

   [Silence after the song ends.]

[Silence as the song starts up again.]

Whatever Thibault was Thibault is:
        like a comet he appears
blazing his stock car through the night sky:
        he circles us, a tetherball caught in orbit

while around and around the pole
        a dancer remembers her appendectomy
as she lap-dances for a happy bachelor
        there by the grace of Fidelity and cocaine.

You see how even change is changed;
        a Skylark, stylish and reliable;
you want something to lean on, lean on
        remembered swallow, remembered meadow:

our sources say there's no such place—
        rest on the nonexistence
time force-feeds the agastache, alyssum,
        when up their little heads they raise

and look around like a periscope, and droop.
        Our sources say they leave no trace.
Thunder Road echoes with roars
        from the quarry owner's sons' RX-7's;

they drown out the sound of boners going Boing
        in the Théâtre Superérotique de Québec
where the dancer spritzes herself and laughs:
        another night, another dent in the appendectomy.

So change is changed, the most powerful force
      is powerless, it goes on and on;
logic will not protect you, you have to have
      stock cars, a rash, false indigo, a rumor.

By the way: I know what you know about me.
      And by I, I mean me, the author, Dan:
I know you know what I did, you spread it:
      I mean the innermost you and me—

the ones inside our brains. I'll have my revenge
      in the form of blossoming amsonia,
amnesiac Orions with their belts undone,
      a hit list, a who's who, a spritz, a marquis.

Tom the stutterer's brother
      had the backhand.
We were doubles partners
      deep inside the quarry.

Camel's Hump was frozen
      on the horizon
snapped mid-undulation.
      Everyone died climbing it.

La Tulip: the feared, hated,
      later embezzler of electricity:
he smashed a fucking asteroid
      past my racket, to Quebec.

Mike's Civic bazookaed Ratt
      to cross-bias La Tulip:
party sled, hedonistic pod,
      our papers in the glove box. . . .

glow-lit, post-match, we drift
      all the way, apparently, to
bug zappers, thunder, G & R. The Strebels
      cough haze and wheeze in the back.

Now the way becomes time,
      and we are still drifting
fresh from a slaughter,
      west, west, west, and west

to a party in a cattle pasture,
       the cattle vaguely suspect.
Mike's father, as you know, deals
       in prize semen. All of this turns out

to be made of paper. Imagine:
       Post-its, notes-to-self,
emotionless as origami.
       Even the backhand, even the match.

Who changed change, die, eightball, tarot, oracle?
        Who put the flux in flux? It was my go-to
when the slipstream slowed to a trickle, hangover cure,
        the reason reason gave the river wonder left behind.

One day I'm looking around in my underwear
        for Paulina Porizkova, now I'm the leech gatherer.
Last week I'm carded trying to buy Coppertone,
        now I'm mistaken for my own pallbearer.

God made change, Daniel; he made change change,
        he made reason reason, bother bother, dust dust.
But why, Sister, why, did he retire before
        he made decrease decrease, limit limit?

Paulina Porizkova and I are having a party. Bill Bixby
        is dancing with Jo Anne Worley. We're all very small,
and very hungry, and lonely, since all our friends
        are dead. We're aphids, alone on a dianthus.

. . . still drifting farther west,
      the clouds in sync,
my thoughts in sync,
      drifting too, and shadows

cast by thoughts, all farther,
      farther west, in sync;
the car, the clouds, the shadows,
      my mind parading slowly

from Charlotte to Ferrisburgh
      with the lake looking on,
and we were looking
      for a homemade sign

we'd find at the end
      of the driveway, by the curb:
a party. Earth brought us here
      even driving the wrong way

across its slowly turning,
      always turning lakes and brooks.
We found the driveway, and
      slowly to the party drove. . . .

Q: Then where did Josh True go?
A: Into the maw, the void, the abyss.

Q: By violence, by illness, by neglect?
A: By none of these causes did he go.

Q: Like a god he strode into storms and water?
A: Neither by lightning nor by drowning.

Q: Then by his beauty, and the gods' jealousy?
A: He looked like Tyne Daly
  wearing an antimatter toupee.
 He did not die valiantly.
  The Earth turned, and he stood still.

Matt crept on Sean
       waiting by the stairs
for Sean to re-emerge
       from the skylit addition,

the parents'-den, lion's-den,
       this is 1986, with Amy,
an astronaut lost in time,
       already headed to oblivion—

Sean led her by the hand,
       the backdrop of what happened
not yet having happened,
       there/not there, as though on layaway;

here is Matt, you know him,
       he's my Star Catcher: baby-blue
sky-blue, robin's-egg bike,
       the brother who drowned in a pool

and resurfaced as the family narrative?
       That Matt. That summer, that poem.
Matt approacheth. Sean, now blown,
       apologizes to him: why?

Laughter as they recap every gag
       and thrust. Neither had,
but Matt had had, a brother.
       Exeunt Sean and Matt.

(continued)

Amy looks at me as though to say,
      You want to go? And leads *me*
to the skylit addition.
      Outside the party, a pattern

Virgil first identified drives
      the cattle, timeless geniuses
of hay and feces, engorged
      until it's time to do their thing:

Mike's dad squeegees another load
      from their zillion-dollar balls,
their mortgaged balls, and overnights
      it to a broker in El Paso.

I owned "East Coker" on cassette.
     We're close to Middlebury now, I pause
and ask my girlfriend how she likes
     the line, *In my beginning is my end.*

She's deep inside her mind; a memory
     of her father, this would have been
the farm in Charlotte, highbush blueberry
     under a canopy of red pines.

He's picking blueberries for pies,
     she rolls in a bed of fragrant needles;
she's nine or ten. Later, by the lake,
     they eat leftovers with lemon juice.

Houses rise and fall, I pause—
     isn't that beautiful? *Are extended, are removed . . .*
And now she's in the backyard
     of the house on Pearl, Reggae Fest weekend:

this was the summer the stars
     could physically be touched,
palmed, released like butterflies
     in the electric heat of the city.

How beautiful it was.
  How beautiful we were,
growing up beside the lake,
  with the west right over there,

back east where we still were,
  and in between, Juniper Island
where we paddled our kayaks,
  got high, tied up, and slept.

Past campfires: little ash-smudge
  flowers in the sand.
Ours is still visible
  from the pier, the balcony.

I swear I was in both places—
  on the balcony, on the beach—
not as a metaphor, I swear,
  but split, or doubled—

that was me and that was me,
  with Sean and Mike and Dave
and the star cattle and Tom
  whose rat-a-tat-tat was shame,

Tom's brother too, his Adonis
  turbo-boost backhand
that rent in twain the Mount Mansfield
  first doubles team, the champions.

At least the island wasn't
         someone's failed attempt
to halt time. It had that in common with
         with Pinhead and the Decentz

and the other bands, whose homegrown new wave
         was Television plus The Clash
minus the Wednesday Reggae Lunch on RUV.
         A dread DJ ripped hits on air.

The balcony, the might-have-been,
        wasn't mine. The party
on the balcony, not mine,
        was mine; the when belongs to nobody.

Josh True was there, his kids like
        little animals around his knee,
my kids in the phase before the phase
        when they're impressionable.

I could touch you, though I
        never touched you, not
until this chain-link conundrum
        made space-time belly flop.

That's me, much farther on in time;
        you lag behind, in bright-blue
flashing neon *I Love You*
        cornflower shadow on snow.

We made out lazily, for hours—
      cf. the underwater scenes in *L'Atalante.*
It was late, our dreams crossed
      and we were nine together, walking home.

It was getting late, and
      you could feel the strain
of all the things that
      hadn't happened yet not happening

or getting ready to happen,
      or the period prior
to their happening ending, the lead-up
      to the prize bull's for-profit climax.

Q: Down the stairs, then rapidly back up?
A: I am the drop in the bucket, the dust on a scale.

Q: You undid God with only a Plymouth Horizon?
A: Plus a breakfast shift and *Four Quartets.*

Q: Which mountains did you face, since you—
A: Since I had two, two sets which I could choose?

Q: Two sets of mountains, pick your side.
A: I chose the Vermont side.
        I set my libido to "poetry."
    Bernie conspired. So did Ben, Jerry,
        Larkin, Lowell, and *Larry King Live.*

Q: *Daniel, lève-toi et récite le Notre Père.*
A: Amnesiac Orions with their belts undone.

Q: *Daniel, répétez: Notre Père, qui es aux cieux—*
A: Matt crept on Sean in the skylit addition.

Q: *Notre Père, qui es aux cieux—Daniel, répétez—*
A: A dread DJ ripped hits on air.

Q: *—Et ne nous induis point en tentation—*
A: Bright-blue flashing neon in snow.
    In a booth in the back, a curtain drawn:
full job, seventy-five. *I Love You*
    written in scar tissue across my throat.

the rock face launched from its chasms
        bright-orange skiers
auroras flashed then drifted
        the skiers were crepe paper

the mountains had a mouth
        and it ate passing airplanes
the conscience of the Adirondacks
        is the sandwort is the tundra yew

a volley of clouds whipped past
        the trees and over the valley
where Mount Mansfield was ready
        with a down-the-line return

and the mountains played this way forever
          volleying to and fro
fronts and storms as though nobody
          planned a homecoming

and you could make them vanish
          and you could make them bashful
and the skiers ran like tears
          and the clouds volleyed were volleyed

back and forth all day
          all day over the valley
Whiteface to Mount Philo
          North Hero to the Gothics

Q: What was downstairs, Dan, in the walk-in?

A: Del Monte; Canadian bacon; Andy Boy; and—

Q: Dan, what was downstairs in the walk-in?

A: Heinz, Vlasic, Hellmann's; and—

Q: Is that why Shooter became a Christian?

A: Not then, not yet: a new baby, an upstairs nursery—

Q: [Shield eyes] Oh God: a tragedy?

A: To the contrary! The way a sunbather
         rolls over and over on terra firma
     the baby rolled over and over and down
             twenty feet into the limbo lap of an azalea.

She steps from cloud to cloud
        in a snow-white cardigan;
her head is the sun, her moonboots
        defy gravity; she is big with child,

but a dragon waits nearby;
        a dragon with a landing strip
that leads into his gut.
        Rewind, rewind, keep going, more, more:

up step on top and view the valley
        Winooski slithering
under the Richmond trestle,
        that's where they built their camp—

"I Shall Be Released"
        before I knew the song
plays over and over
        on an eight-track,

soundtrack of here comes happy
        remembered long after
they'd razed their camp
        and blitzed their family with a ray gun.

He steps from cloud to cloud
        silently embodying the song:
they say everything et cetera,
        every distance et cetera—

Renzo was Feste, the Armageddon jester
     in our Catholic monotone *Twelfth Night*.
Years later he reappeared on *Jeopardy!*,
     blown like a stray balloon by Hurricane Trebek.

Bodhi came home with me, my first fall away.
     I'd told him we were plutocrats
and lived the way a lifeguard lives,
     in the ether, cousins to the horizon.

Since it was Friday, it was pollock.
     He grew up in a Gala orchard near Eureka.
Vermont was more upholstered than I'd said.
     I thought, *Please God, a shout-out from Renzo* . . .

When the pollock appeared he shoveled it down.
     He was/is Kyoto to my Winooski,
hippie-angel-greaser to my malleable morals.
     The still point of the changing channels.

Mariachi noodling was coming from the den
and then it was faux-polka, big-ass
fondant dominatrices with pastel accordions,
Guy & Ralna, Ave Maria, and auf wiedersehen.

I shivered in my bedroom, praying that art
would someday send a ladder from the sky
I could scale and become the love child
of Sylvia Plath, Ozzy, and Alex DeLarge.

I had "Crazy Train" on my Texas Instruments,
and "Daddy," which I recited in the mirror.
Those rape scenes I fast-forwarded, I'm proud to say,
but I slow-mo'd that William Tell ménage à trois.

It worked! Art works if you are otherwise fucked, and try!
Now look at me, almost Ozzy, mansplaining
to my eleven-year-old son the photo
of a Louis Quatorze gilt dildo he found in our cloud.

What happened to Hibbing, Minnesota,
      they asked Dylan.
And Dylan replied: Just time.
      Time is what happened to Hibbing.

Imagine outlasting time,
      appearing on the other side
of it, relieved, like
      Wow What Was That All About?

Imagine outlasting time,
      coming in as from a blizzard,
boots off, coat off, mittens
      frozen into an outstretched hand?

They didn't make coats back then
      like we have now, said Dylan;
there was no crime, and no philosophy—
      people were just too cold back then.

Imagine outlasting time
      to find all of your childhood
pets curled up together in a ball, the cat,
      the fish, the hermit crabs, happy, cozy.

A dream, I had the most horrible dream,
      spake the shepherd fair;
to which his lass replied, no matter now,
      we're here now. Quiet, love.

here I go again into the bone jumpsuit
    detail by detail mortality cosplay

répétez, s'il vous plaît, said my memory to me
    I did and still it said, *Daniel, répétez—*

wring out the dawn, there's a drop of light
    with my name on it, I am thirsty for it

répétez, Daniel; Daniel, répétez—
    répétez s'il vous plaît, Daniel—

Daniel, répétez—

✧✧

III

The Math Campers' Masque

It's Friday! Linus and Lucy
      are going apeshit on the Internet!
Fucking Woodstock looks as though
      he's going to explode with joy!

Charlie Brown, cautiously carefree
      karate kicks the air,
while Snoopy, serenity itself
      though denied dog pleasures

like licking filthy laundry
      looking for a chicken-stock-soaked
apron, Snoopy is happy!
      They gather, one and all

"around the bonfire, the association
      of man and woman, in daunsinge,
signifying matrimonie—a dignified
      and commodious sacrament."

A BOWER in a hot summer forest. The smell of pines mixes with lake water. Across the lake, a LIBERAL ARTS COLLEGE.

MATH CAMPERS drift across the lake in yellow inner tubes, linking arms as a group, floating together on the water, before dissolving into individual yellow points on the fringes of the lake.

A PEACH TREE blooms, weeks early.

In a building across the lake, JANET TWIST, a dean, and KYLE CONSTANTINOPLE, a philosopher, bring their long affair to an end. Gestures between them suggest passion long mellowed into affection.

A MAN and a WOMAN, long married, recline on the forest floor, discussing the nature of passing time.

MAN.

We made this grove when we closed our eyes.
If we open them, snows freeze
And zombies swearing patriotic oaths will rise.

WOMAN.

We made this bower out of our desire.
I held your head under the water.
Remember your pleasure when I forced you under?

And then I shaved your head when you'd been bad.
And then I cut you with my blade
And promises were made

And promises were made on 75th Street
In the unseasonable summer heat
And it was then that that was that.

MAN.

I had a dream last night, nested inside another dream. To get
out of the first dream I had to pass into a new dream. From the
new dream, I looked back on the first dream and called that
dream reality.

In the first dream, *L*, age fourteen, took the train into Boston
for the day, to shop for vintage comic books in the stores near
Kenmore Square.

When he returned that afternoon on the 5:40 train, he was a man. He had grown up. He looked at me with a sarcastic expression: hadn't I realized that was why he'd gone into Boston?

"That was the point," he said: "That was the point of going, Dad."

In the second dream, I wake up from the first. It's the same day; L is arriving on the 5:40 train, which we hear pulling into the station from our bedroom. L calls out to us as he enters the house. His voice is deeper. He is twenty-six, I somehow know; and yet I can tell from his expression, his absence of pity, his totally casual air upon entering our house, that we've aged along with him. We're twelve years older in that single day. We're fifty-nine; the mirror confirms it.

In the middle of the second dream, I recall the first. I dream that the first dream was reality. I am relieved. That is not my face in the mirror. My face is still young-enough-looking, my muscles are still toned, my hair, though getting sparse on top, is still full and unruly.

L, a thriving and healthy young person, aged twenty-six, goes up to his room, gets into his little boy's bed, and falls asleep.

THE MATH CAMPERS (in unison).

We've measured out the summer
With the math we've learned so far.

(continued)

If we want a longer summer,
We have to practice harder.

Love is a figure
Divided by another figure.
The lovers looking everywhere
For answers are the answers.

THE MATH CAMPERS (singing together while drifting apart).

We're tied to stars and prone to fever.
It's not yet time for us to fall in love;
It's not too late to vow we'll never.

MAN, calling out to THE MATH CAMPERS.

On the Internet,
I saw a man ingesting shit
On a fetish site:
Stay prepubescent!

I saw a cartoon mule
Blowing
A cartoon otter!

THE MATH CAMPERS, in tears, are called to shore, where their
mothers await them, holding towels. Their empty inner tubes
rock gently in the aimless drift of the lake water.

THE PEACH TREE.

> Too fucking soon, you narcissist!
> Too fucking soon! The basics first:
> You don't fast-forward to ingesting shit.
> You go to the mall first on a group date.
> You sit around by the phone and wait.
> You find an ally or a spy and you collaborate.
> You offer, first, your heart.
> You offer up your heart to eat.
> You watch as they gnaw your heart to the pit.
> Your heart is a pit. He spits, she spits.

MAN.

> So strange: so bitter, yet so sweet.

WOMAN.

> Pick his ripest fruit.

MAN.

> Now what?

WOMAN.

> Now listen to the Dean's heartbeat:

(continued)

DEAN JANET TWIST.

>My heart beats, you interpret it.
>By the waters where
>We began our affair
>You chose, I chose,
>Its sell-by date.
>Your dick hasn't worked in years;
>Now even the poetry's prose.

KYLE CONSTANTINOPLE.

>Ours were the last hearts on Earth allowed to sample a love so
>total that the poets, hearing of our love, came rushing to the
>upstairs conference room, to hear those ancient vows recited
>once more, before they were gone forever.

>Remember? It was the fall of '95, my tenure case had been
>decided in the affirmative.

DEAN JANET TWIST.

>We taught them how real lovers live.
>It was a cross-curricular initiative.
>It was a moment so transformative
>We used it in our capital drive.

MAN, calling out to **TWIST** and **CONSTANTINOPLE.**

>You who control our work and pay,
>Tell us, for we are lost,

For we are lost in the forest:
Oh, must we mean what we say?

WOMAN.

They can't hear you. They are in the past.

Where they are you and I
are strangers.
Where they are you and I
are younger.

See, even now they vanish into retirement.
They are premonitory ghosts.

The MAN and WOMAN share a peach, alternating bites and
tenderly wiping each other's faces. They were given one day, a
day of no fixed duration, years long; and now they see the day
begin to end.

THE PEACH TREE winces every time they take a bite.

THE MATH CAMPERS, high-fiving and loudly exclaiming,
remove their shoes and return to their inner tubes, floating
in a summer made suddenly endless by new methods of
multiplication! They have found a way out of time! Their
summer will never end. They will now solve a lifelong, endless
problem, many blackboards long.

Two boys kiss and laugh in a cove by the old paint shop.

(continued)

THE MATH CAMPERS' chorus fades, first barely audible, then inaudible, as the campers float away on the lake.

THE MATH CAMPERS' CHORUS

A mayfly waking up at dawn
Dies when the sun goes down;
A tortoise on an English lawn
[inaudible] its owner's son's son's son.

In the elastic interval between
Snack and Nonlinear Equations
[inaudible] we learn
We divvy up [inaudible]

[inaudible] [the sound of katydids]
[barn swallows overhead] friends
Divide by multiply [moon]
[moon] [moon] [moon] [moon]

FINIS.

IV

Over & Over

For our sons

winter moth I put your body on
        and I was happy with the armor
flight was both possible and necessary
        since I was light, brittle and miniature

flight was both happy and panicky
        now that I was inside your body
my awareness stretching far beyond
        my wingspan and erratic decision-making pattern

I was now entirely akin to myself
        now I resembled myself both inside and out
who's the guy with the new temporality
        of a moth's life, only a day or two

in his resplendent, powdery body
        before annihilation minus zero
when January in one enormous puff
        exhaled ice across the landscape?

like a child seen getting used to a man's body
      seen when least he wishes to be seen
seen walking in when he would like to be
      conveyed invisibly to his seat in math

or like the melody hastening itself away
      in "Honey Hi," the sweetness
ticking its own lifespan away
      jittery, alert, despite my new blue peacoat

hold your hand up to the screen—
        hold your hand up to the page—
cover this stanza up just so
        cover these lines up with your hands

just so I held my hand a minute ago
        to block what I was writing
and possibly to mirror
        your hand as it mimicked mine

or will, if you hold your hand up
        to the screen, or to the page—
but this was years ago, now—
        this moment unfolding now was years ago

my awareness seems to extend this day
        past the trap my body set for me
past its small, pitiful adjustments
        of head here wings here antennae here

what does it matter, the head and wings
        and antennae if my awareness
soars over the tops of the pines
        with its spiny flowers still green

like a drone flown by a teenage pilot
        over the rooftops, silent yawp
past near meadows over the Stop & Shop
        its dragonfly landing gear ready

now it zooms in on the roots which grip
        the soil and feed on its decay
your hand and mine at the same angle
        you there, in the future, fleeing me

:if the reader will please turn over
      her hands to expose her palms
I will do so too and together, stranger
      together we shall contemplate enormity

He wrote to me again

He wrote to me again in a dream. A mild winter, a false start
for the daffodils and for the fragrant hyacinths, whose green
was suicidal in the beds and near the hedges

and for the snowdrops whose dainty
       necks bend under the weight of the flower
doomed when they hear their name to misunderstand
       their natures, bowed, ruined by one frigid day

Why do they talk this way? I asked him.

The flowers? he replied.

The poets, I replied.

He wrote to me again in a dream. *Koyaanisqatsi*-style, all life
was time-lapsed into pattern. He emerged from out of the
pattern but was not entirely human. He was more like a string
of Christmas lights around a human body.

In this form, more pattern than human, he approached me.
And then I saw, beside him, another pattern: he was walking a
little dog, a small constellation of lights tracing the shape of a
little low-to-the-ground, comical dog, a dachshund or beagle.
You could see just from the ways the constellations of their
bodies interplayed, they loved each other: the outline of a man
and the outline of a dog, moving as one being across the field
towards me.

Why do they talk this way? I asked.

The poets? he replied.

The flowers, I replied.

they speak a language we can understand
      "of woe and worry and ruined beauty"—
that's why they speak this way
      you'd have a poem rhyme rhizome?

The poets, you mean?

The flowers, I mean.

if the reader will now step away from the page
        if the reader will now step away from the screen
together we will ponder who imagined whom
        and downstairs, start a new pot of coffee

if the reader will please wait to have begun
      this poem until 11:54 p.m., it will sync
up perfectly with midnight—wait, wait—
      the word *Forlorn* on the stroke of midnight

He wanted to meet me, but our element was time. He approached me, where I was standing, years later; and I approached him where he stood, but he was too far in the past.

We shared the illusion of approach, as on a treadmill. He walked towards me on his treadmill, and I walked towards him on mine.

Soon we were sprinting towards each other, faster but no closer, faster, faster, but never closer, trapped in the eternal loop of the machine.

His poor dog! His little legs were not meant for such a strain. He was cross with his master; he was exhausted and cross with his master.

ten past midnight on my single day, well past
        the midpoint of my life, my body was finally
what I intended it to be. Mr. Chrysalis!
        your formality disgusts me. Empty promises and goo

I suspect you are thinking of your sons, I said.

—You suspect correctly.

What aspect of their lives most worries you?

—That I can see inside of them.

Why does it worry you to see inside of them?

—Because I see myself inside of them.

What makes you certain it's you?

[dramatic pause, uncomfortably prolonged]

[in the background, a twin-engine plane appears in the sky]

—I am wearing an ID tag. I check theirs against mine, the numbers match, and so we are the same person.

[the plane lurches suddenly, then drops; there is an enormous explosion, then a plume of smoke]

in his sweet rebellion I see my own
　　　in his trying on for the sake of trying on
the highway leading only to other highways
　　　　the GPS already certain where we're headed

since all its prophecies are memories—
　　　what is this? O what is this new thing?
said I to my body, said he
　　　to his body, what side effect of passing time is this?

But our bodies were speechless, in unison.

      We sat in the International House of Speechlessness.

Our bodies cried to each other speechlessly,

         as time stole one after another minute together.

Our bodies cried out to each other speechlessly,

         as more time carried little bits of us away.

Then we laughed the family laugh, to find

         ourselves the specials on the menu we perused.

Coda: Stonington

On the deck upstairs, I read about
      the deck upstairs. In the daybed
I read about the daybed. In the books
      I read I read about the books I read.

⁙

High up, all night, I thought about
      my sons, how when they wake
I will be finishing this line:
      my night their day from here on out.

⁙

Birds, check. First light. Sunrise.
      Pole vaulting all night long.
My outline splayed on the guest bed
      where Mary McCarthy stayed.

⁙

The sponsors: the bats, the bottles;
      The milk-glass tabletop, the china cup.
The *Santorini Guide* and smiling lads from 1982.
      A tin mini–license plate read "Jim."

⁙

In a book on one of the shelves
      I left a copy of this poem
changed slightly since that night
      changed crucially yet slightly

⁙

(continued)

since the night I lay on the star deck
    and made my body an angel
in the warm September night
    above the Sound and its bright buoys

the way I did when I was a small child
    in a snowbank in my zippered snowsuit
you can find this poem inside a book
    on the shelves in the hidden study

three to the left of the *Santorini Guide*
    though when you find it you will see
the poem changed slightly, crucially—
    because, you know why: because time.

The
Math
Campers

Johnson / Shelburne / Ripton,
Vermont, Spring 2019

A mayfly born at the break of dawn
dies when the sun goes down.
A tortoise on an English lawn
outlives his master's son's son's son.

An ancient shark shakes off another century;
eerie and pristine, a fetal dolphin,
a steamship, and a sea anemone
hang near her, lifeless in the jellied ocean.

This shark read over Milton's shoulder.
In her extreme old age, she'll stare
eye to eye, into a skyscraper's foyer,
at gilled, amphibious corporate lawyers.

The big night stares us down from space;
we figured we would have more years;
annihilation in her prom dress
greets her platonic date, despair;

the black hole poses for her picture
wearing a coronet of stars;
a glacier, like a mountain, only bigger,
rides southward on its own shed tears;

the deserts parched for centuries
put on their snorkel gear;
scorpions write their obituaries;
a cactus curtsies, then disappears.

First in their class, the lichens
sprawl like a rash or a blush
on the face of a glacial erratic.
A thunderclap deafens the marsh.

This who's who comes from all over:
a thawed field is a gold mine,
an uproar over winterberries,
chitchat along the power lines. . . .

What happens happened later earlier;
what happens earlier happened later.
Now frost is a shallow passenger
and biohazards ride the white-tailed deer.

A beetle polishes its psychedelic shell.
Fireflies splatter-paint the night.
The keeper's Honda's battery failed
parked near the cemetery gate.

The cemetery overlooks the brook
that blazed the highway's route.
A hurricane washes out the highway.
The cemetery seesaws on its bank

then makes a break for the valley.
Caskets line up for the slip-n-slide.
A collarbone surfboards down the alley.
Through the mudslide we humans wade.

In April, when the animals
In April when the animals emerge
One by one from their holes
As from an advent calendar

To meet their awaiting identities
The mouse shimmies into her fur
The patch of blue expects its jay
Hello chipmunk I am nervousness

In April when the animals
In April when the animals emerge
As from their office cubicles
And the world wakes up, enlarged—

The spring held all its dividends,
then shed them like confetti;
home in Vermont last weekend,
I saw biofuel silos in the country,

farmers returning to farming,
asparagus, ramps, hemp
new ferns along the paths unfurling,
and robins waking sleepily.

In middle school, if two boys
want to kiss, or hold hands, they can;
sixth-graders learn sea-level rise
and march with their friends against guns;

The hills say there's no single way
to be, up here, this time of spring:
swimmable water in the valley,
snow on Mount Mansfield still falling.

In Greensboro, the Saabs
transformed to Priuses
crustier than the ones in cities,
driven by nurses and heiresses.

Near Caspian Lake one day
Chief Justice Rehnquist at his summer house
swore Stephen Breyer in, only
a part-time village clerk to witness.

The Circus Camp patches its tents;
the Farm Camp rouses on the hill;
a goat behind a wire fence
prepares to be clumsily milked.

Hard problems at the Math Camp wait
all winter for solutions;
engorged sums hibernate
and dream of consolation;

A raft dry-docked through winter
gets its feet wet and waits
for July, when the Math Campers
arrive, to stare at the stars and calculate

the absolute value of fifteen
or how the summer might expand
and prove eternal by division
of days into hours, minutes, seconds;

they're factoring love in suddenly
and measuring how the stars in pairs
create the sky's geometry,
and measuring their hearts' spheres,

skew lines of who they are and were;
they know, year over year, you grow
by comparing consecutive summers
and expressing them in a ratio.

Now, in the interval between
dodge ball and snack, the Math Campers
back-of-the-envelope equations
they must solve to make the summer longer.

They've meted out the summer
with the math they've done so far;
if they want a longer summer,
oh, they'll have to practice harder:

For every correct answer, one more hour;
a furlough from the changing leaves.
The daisies cheer from the bleachers
and bumblebees gossip about love.

Rationalists will say they failed.
Fall came and bulldozed the bees.
The daisies saw their heads explode
and parents returned in their SUVs.

The raft was dragged to a frozen lawn.
The October stars withdrew
into relations of their own.
Ice strangled the bright yarrow.

Black Adder has a restraining order
against Hyssop: fucking psycho
arrived in a three-wheeler
and did donuts in the meadow;

An astronaut unzips his suit
and masturbates to the turning Earth,
while distant galaxies ejaculate
in acid trips of death and birth;

first in his class, he spends the day
on beating off and solo chess,
and writing in his diary
"I gave up Earth for fucking *this*—"

an organ on the TV mass
plays all day for company;
the wonders of the Universe
turn into drudgery;

the Universe, first in its class,
elaborates its origin
in the enormity of space;
light finds its lost horizon

then vanishes in ecstasy;
a dust-cyclone undoes the sun
and kills our Opportunity.
The little rover lost its friends.

First in his class, he toiled hard
on valedictory remarks
for his own graduation:
"My battery is low. It's getting dark."

Bloom (II)

David Teng Olsen, Mural, 2017

At sunset, this October,
      I picked some Nippon daisies,
the last flower to flower,
      a verb named for its noun.

The weather was all indoors.
      A Page solo plus Michelangelo
enameled in cerulean, tangles
      of what looked like instant ramen,

a heavy barge in the surf offshore,
      a spindly zeppelin down, the scene
split by an architectural birch
      crisscrossed by laser blasts.

Dave added the sky one day,
      then blew our heads apart
by denying it had ever been a sky.
      A spider creature was our sons.

Their hair entangled meant
      they would now never be apart,
not their whole lives wandering
      in a world itself worryingly

wandering who knows where.

    Look, there's a friendly bloom;
look, a vivisectionist, a severed wrist.

    These thoughts our house had had about us.

Acknowledgments

Many thanks to the editors of the following publications, where these poems, sometimes in altered forms, first appeared:

"Years ago, our sons were born . . ." (*West Branch*)

"He asked me my happiest memory . . ." (*West Branch*)

"I owned, East Coker, . . ." (*The Yale Review*)

"How beautiful it was . . ." (*The Yale Review*)

"The balcony, the might-have-been . . ." (*The Yale Review*)

"We made out lazily, for hours . . ." (*The Yale Review*)

"He was writing an autumn journal . . ." (*The Yale Review*)

"That fall, he had been invited . . ." (*The Yale Review*)

"He patrolled the Sound in his mind . . ." (*The Yale Review*)

"It was already November when he wrote again . . ." (*The Yale Review*)

"Coda: Stonington" (*The Yale Review*)

"Tom the stutterer's brother . . ." (*The New Yorker*)

"Who changed change, die, eightball, tarot, oracle? . . ." (*The New Yorker*)

"Sitting in a swivel chair . . ." (*The Sewanee Review*)

"If you want to make it to the moon . . ." (*The Sewanee Review*)

"The gap kept getting filled in . . ." (*The Sewanee Review*)

"*The rock face launched from its chasms . . .*" (*The Sewanee Review*)

"What happened to Hibbing, Minnesota . . ." (*The Sewanee Review*)

"Half in, half out of my dream . . ." (*The New York Review of Books*)

"Bloom (II)" (Academy of American Poets)

"My awareness seems to extend this day . . ." (Knopf Poem-a-Day)

The illustration on the jacket is from a handmade periodical assembled by a group of English teenagers during one summer in the 1870s. It is captioned "My Lady in Waiting" and is unsigned.

"Bloom" and "Bloom (II)" describe a mural in our house, painted by the artist David Teng Olsen, and depicting, in surreal, sometimes delightful, sometimes disturbing ways, scenes from our family life.

The title "Must We Mean What We Say?" is borrowed from the famous essay and book by Stanley Cavell, and intended to reframe his famous question in terms of poetry. Poets borrow the language, and with it the emotions, of their ancestors. They say things they don't mean, or they say things they mean in codes and in guises. Poets deflect sincerity onto strangers and shadows.

I am indebted for the tone of section I of that poem to the English-language narrator of Chris Marker's film *Sans Soleil*.

The epigraph, from Henry James's *What Maisie Knew*, was suggested to me by Garth Greenwell.

Much of the poem was written while I was staying at the Merrill Apartment in Stonington, Connecticut. My thanks to everyone at the James Merrill House, and especially to Sally Wood.

"The Math Campers" was written while I was staying as writer-in-residence at the Vermont Studio Center and, a week later, at the Bread Loaf Environmental Writers' Conference. My thanks to Megan Mayhew Bergman. Parts of the poem were delivered at the 2019 Phi Beta Kappa exercises of Harvard University, and written for that occasion. Thanks to Hopi Hoekstra.

Thanks, as ever, to my editor, Deborah Garrison; to Todd Portnowitz at Knopf; to my wife, Annie Adams; and to my colleagues and students at Wellesley College.

This book is dedicated to Frank Bidart, my friend, colleague, and mentor. My work would not have existed without his.

A NOTE ON THE TYPE

The text in this book was set in Miller, a transitional-style typeface designed by Matthew Carter (b. 1937) with assistance from Tobias Frere-Jones and Cyrus Highsmith of the Font Bureau. Modeled on the roman family of fonts popularized by Scottish type foundries in the nineteenth century, Miller is named for William Miller, founder of the Miller & Richard foundry of Edinburgh.

Composed by North Market Street Graphics,
Lancaster, Pennsylvania

Printed and bound by Friesens,
Altona, Manitoba

Book design by Pei Loi Koay